ICAEW Financial Rep

First edition 2008

ISBN 9780 7517 4610 5

British Library Cataloguing-in-Publication Data

A catalogue record for this book is available from the British Library

Published by

BPP Learning Media Ltd, BPP House, Aldine Place, London W12 8AA

www.bpp.com/learningmedia

Printed in Great Britain by WM Print

Your learning materials, published by BPP Learning Media Ltd,
are printed on paper sourced from sustainable, managed forests.

Welcome to BPP Learning Media's ICAEW **Passcards** for the **Financial Reporting** Paper.

- They **save you time**. Important topics are summarised for you.

- They incorporate **diagrams** to kick start your memory.

- They follow the overall **structure** of the ICAEW Study Manuals, but BPP Learning Media's ICAEW **Passcards** are not just a condensed book. Each card has been separately designed for clear presentation. Topics are self contained and can be grasped visually.

- ICAEW **Passcards** are **just the right size** for pockets, briefcases and bags.

- ICAEW **Passcards focus on the exams** you will be facing.

Run through the complete set of **Passcards** as often as you can during your final revision period. The day before the exam, try to go through the **Passcards** again! You will then be well on your way to passing your exams.

Good luck!

1: Reporting framework

Topic List

IASB *Framework*

Regulatory framework

Convergence process

Small-and medium-sized entities

Fair presentation

Ethical and professional issues

In order to fully appreciate IAS/IFRS it is important to understand the conceptual and regulatory framework which has produced these Standards.

IASB Framework

IASB Framework	Regulatory framework	Convergence process	Small-and medium-sized entities	Fair presentation	Ethical and professional issues

Objectives of financial statements

Financial position
- Balance sheet

Financial performance
- Income statement
- Cash flow statement
- Statement of recognised income and expense

Changes in financial performance
- Income statement
- Statement of recognised income and expense
- Cash flow statement
- Statement of changes in equity
- Notes to the financial statements
- Directors' report

Accruals ← **Underlying assumptions** → Going concern

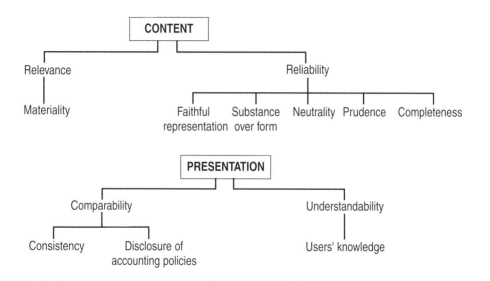

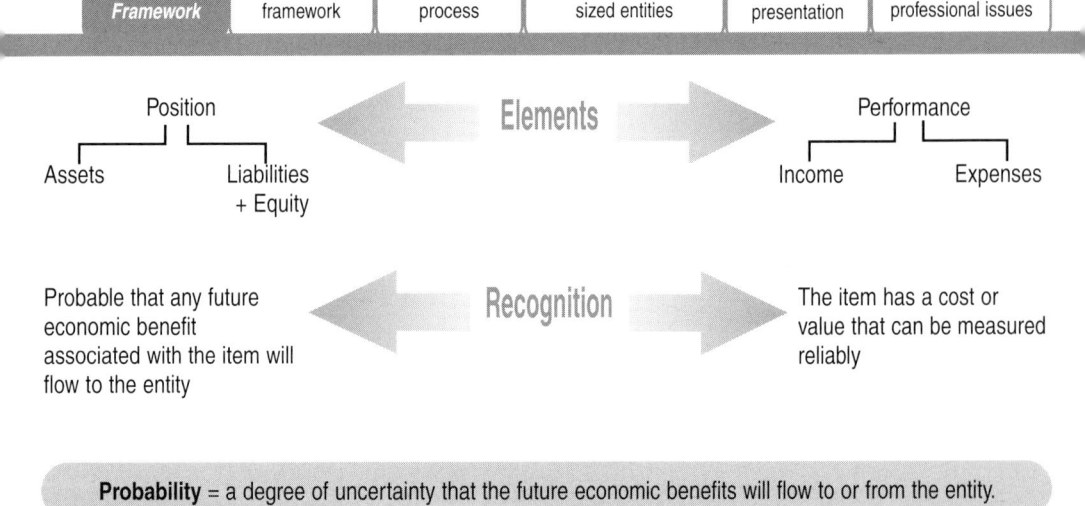

Position

Assets — Liabilities + Equity

← **Elements** →

Performance

Income — Expenses

Probable that any future economic benefit associated with the item will flow to the entity

← **Recognition** →

The item has a cost or value that can be measured reliably

Probability = a degree of uncertainty that the future economic benefits will flow to or from the entity.

Measurement

Historic cost
(acquisition value)

Current cost (amount if
acquired currently)

How should an item
be valued?

Present value (present
discounted value of future
net cash inflows item
expected to generate)

Realisable (settlement)
value (amount selling
in current state)

Financial capital maintenance

Profit is earned if the financial amount of the net assets at the end of a period exceeds the financial amount of net assets at the beginning of a period after excluding any distributions to, and contributions from, owners during the period.

Can be measured in either nominal monetary units of units of constant purchasing power.

Physical capital maintenance

Profit is earned if the physical productive capacity (or operating capacity) of the entity at the end of the period exceeds the physical productive capacity at the beginning of the period, after excluding any distributions to and contributions from, owners during the period. This concept requires the current cost basis of measurement.

The selection of the measurement bases and concept of capital maintenance together determine the accounting model used.

Regulatory framework

International Accounting Standards

European Union

Other

Listed companies to comply with IAS from 2005.

National laws

- Take precedence over IASs/IFRSs

OECD

- Undertakes its own research into accounting standards, via *ad hoc* working groups, issuing guidelines for members

Stock Exchange

National Listing Rules to be complied with by listed companies.

The IASB issued 41 IASs. Standards are now called IFRS and eight IFRSs have been issued so far. The procedure for issuing an IFRS can be summarised as follows.

1. During the early stages of a project, the IASB may establish an **Advisory Committee** to give advice on issues arising in the project. Consultation with the Advisory Committee and the Standards Advisory Council occurs throughout the project.

2. IASB may develop and publish **Discussion Documents** for public comment.

3. Following the receipt and review of comments, IASB would develop and publish an **Exposure Draft** for public comment.

4. Following the receipt and review of comments, the IASB would issue a final **International Financial Reporting Standard**.

Convergence process

Barriers to harmonisation

- Language
- Different purposes of financial reporting
- Different legal systems
- Different user groups
- Needs of developing countries
- Nationalism
- Cultural differences
- Unique circumstances, eg hyperinflation
- Lack of strong accountancy bodies

Advantages of harmonisation

- Investors can compare results of different companies internationally
- Advantages for multinationals include:
  - Easier investment
  - Easier compliance
  - Easier to transfer accounting staff across national boundaries
- Governments of developing countries can adopt International Standards for internal use
- Easier to promote cross border trade
- Large global accounting firms find multinational companies easier to audit

Progress with harmonisation

IASB

- In May 2000 agreed with IOSCO to allow companies that follow 30 IASs to obtain corporate funds via listing on any IOSCO member exchange.

- IAS Improvements Project: changes made in December 2003 to 13 IASs to eliminate alternatives and conflicts.

- FASB Convergence Project: aims to remove differences from US GAAP. Objective is to remove requirement for US GAAP reconciliation altogether by 2009.

- IASB and FASB developing common conceptual framework.

EU AND OTHER

- EU Directives have affected company law and reporting substantially, and this will continue.

- Since 2005, consolidated accounts of listed companies have been required to comply with IAS. Other countries to adopt IFRS include Australia, Jamaica, New Zealand, Russia and Tanzania.

- The UK is well underway with a **Convergence Project** to compare UK Standards with IASs.

Small-and medium-sized entities (SMEs)

Most companies are **small** ie owned and managed by one person or family.

Should there be two GAAPs?

- Simple for smaller companies
- More detailed for longer ones

In the UK, the **FRSSE** was developed for small companies, ie companies below certain legally defined limits.

Discussion Paper and Exposure Draft

- **DP** published in June 2004. Standards for SMEs should be a **modified version of full IFRS**
- Focus on **non-public accountability** rather than size
- **Each IFRS** would have its **SME equivalent**. SME Standards would **change in line with IFRS**
- **Pick and mix approach**, ie entities could follow IFRS in some areas and IFRS for SMEs in others
- **ED** published in 2007
- **ED** aims to provide a simplified, self-contained set of principles for smaller, non-listed entities
- Removes topics not relevant to SMEs and removes choices

International

- IAS 1 requires financial statements to **present fairly** the position and performance of a company
- This will usually be true if IFRS is adhered to
- Departure from IFRS only allowed in very rare cases where financial statements would be misleading

UK

- CA 85 requires that financial statements give a **true and fair view**
- True = factual accuracy
  Fair = objective and unbiased
- If compliance with SSAP/FRS would not give true and fair view: statutory 'true and fair override'
- CA requires disclosure of:
  - particulars of departure
  - reasons
  - financial effect

Ethical and professional issues

A code of moral principles that people follow with respect to what is right or wrong

Not necessarily enforced by law

Ethical systems

- **Personal ethics** – eg deriving from upbringing or political or religious beliefs

- **Professional ethics** – eg medical ethics

- **Organisation culture**

- **Organisation systems** – may be in a formal code reinforced by the overall statement of values

Two approaches

- **Compliance based** – ensures that the company acts within the letter of the law. Violations are prevented, detected and punished.

- **Integrity based** – combines a concern for the law with an emphasis on managerial responsibility for ethical behaviours. Strives to define companies' guiding values, aspirations and pattern of thought and conduct.

Code of ethics

This lays out ICAEW's rules stating the ethics and behaviour required by all members and **students**. Guidance is in the form of **fundamental principles** (see below), specific guidance statements and explanatory notes.

Integrity	Members should be straightforward and honest in all business and professional relationships.
Objectivity	Members should not allow bias, conflicts of interest or undue influence of others to override professional or business judgements.
Professional competence and due care	Members have a continuing duty to maintain professional knowledge and skill at a level required to ensure that a client or employer receives competent professional service based on current developments in practice, legislation and techniques. Members should act diligently and in accordance with applicable technical and professional standards when providing professional services.
Confidentiality	Members should respect the confidentiality of information acquired as a result of professional and business relationships and should not disclose any such information to third parties without proper or specific authority or unless there is a legal or professional right or duty to disclose. Confidential information acquired as a result of professional and business relationships should not be used for the personal advantage of members or third parties.
Professional behaviour	Members should comply with relevant laws and regulations and should avoid any action that discredits the profession.

Compliance with the fundamental principles may potentially be threatened by a broad range of circumstances:

Threats
■ **Self-interest** threat eg financial interests, incentive compensation arrangements, undue dependence on fees
■ **Self-review** threat eg data being reviewed by the same person responsible for preparing it
■ **Advocacy** threat eg acting as an advocate on behalf of an assurance client in litigation or disputes with third parties
■ **Familiarity** threat eg former partner of the firm being a director or officer of the client
■ **Intimidation** threat eg threat of dismissal or replacement, being pressured to reduce inappropriately the extent of work performed in order to reduce fees

Three categories of safeguards exist: those created by regulations, those created by the individual and those created in the work environment.

Regulations	**Work environment**

- ICAEW code/IFAC code
- ISAs
	- Recruitment procedures
	- Appropriate disciplinary processes
	- Leadership that stresses the importance of ethical behaviour
	- Policies and procedures to implement and monitor the
	  – quality of employee performance
	  – quality control of engagements
	- Using different partners and teams for the provision of non-audit services to assurance clients
	- Discussing ethical issues with those charged with governance
	- Consultation with another professional accountant

Individual	
- Complying with continuing professional development requirements - Keeping records of contentious issues and decisions - Using an independent mentor - Maintaining contact with legal advisers and professional bodies	

Independence

Independence of mind is the state of mind that permits the provision of an opinion without being affected by influences that compromise professional judgement, allowing an individual to act with integrity, and exercise objectivity and professional scepticism.

Independence in appearance is the avoidance of facts and circumstances that are so significant that a reasonable and informed third party, having knowledge of all relevant information, including safeguards applied, would reasonably conclude a firm's, or a member's, integrity, objectivity or professional scepticism had been compromised.

Aim is to help firms and members:

1 Identify threats to independence

2 Evaluate whether threats are insignificant

3 If not, identify and apply safeguards

Financial interests · Loans and guarantees · Close business relationships · Litigation · Family and personal relationships · **Threats to independence** · Fees · Employment connections with assurance client · Gifts/hospitality · Provision of multiple services · Long association

Notes

2: Reporting financial performance

Topic List

Financial accounting material

IAS12 *Income Taxes*

IAS 14 *Segment Reporting*

IFRS 8 *Operating Segments*

IAS 24 *Related Party Disclosure*

Other financial and operational information

UK GAAP comparison

This chapter covers additional material from that studied in Financial Accounting *to help you to prepare useful financial statements. We start with a reminder of the formats for financial statements and then move onto additional areas.*

Balance sheet (IAS 1)

	20X2	20X1
Assets		
Non-current assets		
Property, plant & equipment	×	×
Goodwill	×	×
Other intangible assets	×	×
Investments in associates	×	×
Available-for-sale investments	—	×
Current assets		
Inventories	×	×
Trade receivables	×	×
Other current assets	×	×
Cash and cash equivalents	—	—
Total assets	×	×
Equity and liabilities		
Equity attributable to equity holders of the parent	×	×
Share capital	×	×
Other reserves	×	×
Retained earnings	—	—
Minority interest	×	×
Total equity	×	×
Non current liabilities	—	—
Long-term borrowings	×	×
Deferred tax	×	×
Long-term provisions	×	×
Total non-current liabilities	×	×
Current liabilities	×	×
Trade and other payables	—	—
Short term borrowings	×	×
Current portion of long-term borrowings	×	×
Current tax payable	×	×
Short-term provisions	×	—
Total current liabilities	—	×
Total equity and liabilities	×	×

Legend (side tabs):

- UK GAAP comparison — IAS 24 Related Party Disclosures
- Other financial and operational information — IFRS 8 Operating Segments — IAS 14 Segment Reporting
- Income Taxes — IAS 12
- Financial accounting material

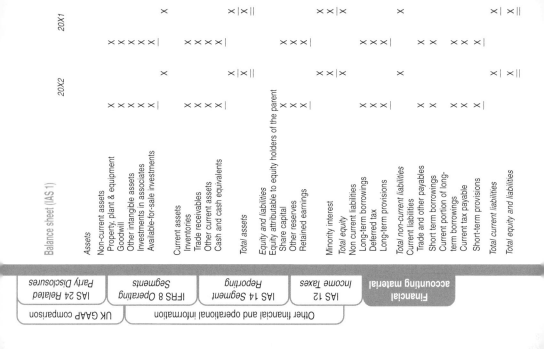

Income statement (IAS 1)

	20X2	20X1
Revenue	X	X
Cost of sales	(X)	(X)
Gross profit	X	X
Other income	X	X
Distribution costs	(X)	(X)
Administrative expenses	(X)	(X)
Other expenses	(X)	(X)
Finance costs	(X)	(X)
Share of profit of associates*	X	X
Profit before tax	X	X
Income tax expense	(X)	(X)
Profit for the period	X	X
Attributable to:		
Equity holders of the parent	X	X
Minority interest	X	X
	X	X

* After tax and minority interests in the associates

A not-for-profit entity would prepare a Statement of Financial Position (balance sheet) and Statement of Financial Performance (income statement).

2: Reporting financial performance

IAS 8 *Accounting Policies, Changes in Accounting Estimates and Errors*

Should include all items of income and expense for the period (ie not hidden in reserves) unless an IAS requires/permits otherwise. **The revised IAS outlaws extraordinary items**.

Accounting policies

Accounting policies are the specific principles, bases, conventions, rules and practices applied by an entity in preparing and presenting statements.

An entity follows extant Standards and Interpretations when determining its accounting policies.

In the absence of a Standard or Interpretation covering a specific transaction, other event or condition, management uses its judgement to develop an accounting policy which results in information that is relevant and reliable, considering in the following order:

- Standards or Interpretations dealing with similar and related issues

- The *Framework* definitions and recognition criteria

- Other national GAAPs based on a similar conceptual framework (providing the treatment does not conflict with extant Standards, Interpretations or the *Framework*)

Changes in accounting policy

Only allowed if:

- Required by Standard or Interpretation
- The change will provide more relevant or reliable information about events or transactions

Accounting treatment:

- Restate prior year I/S and B/S
- Restate opening balance of retained earnings
- Include as second line of statement of changes in equity
- Show effect on prior period at foot of prior year SOCIE

Changes in accounting estimates

Apply **prospectively**, ie in the current period (and future periods if also affected)

Prior period errors

Omissions from and misstatements in the entity's financial statements for one or more periods.

Correct material prior period errors retrospectively in the first set of financial statements authorised for issue after their discovery.

- Restate comparative amounts for each prior period presented in which the error occurred

- Restate the opening balances of assets, liabilities and equity for the earliest prior period presented

- Include any adjustment to opening equity as the second line of the statement of changes in equity

- Disclose the nature of the error and the amount of the correction to prior periods for each line item in each period affected

Where it is impracticable to determine the period-specific effects or the cumulative effect of the error, the entity corrects the error from the earliest period/date practicable (and discloses that fact).

IAS 12 *Income Taxes*

IAS 12 covers current tax. Current tax is fairly easy.

Tax charge	
Current tax	X
Under-/over-statement of prior periods	X/(X)
Share of tax of associates	X
	X

Current tax: an estimate of income tax payable for the current year

Under-/over-statement of prior periods: as the income tax charge on taxable profits is only an estimate, there may be adjustments required in the next accounting period

IAS 14 *Segment Reporting*

Reasons for segment information

- Explains factors which have contributed to results
- Users can compare results of different products
- Users can compare performance with competitors
- Users can assess future risks and rewards

- IAS 14 only applies to entities whose equity or debt is traded on public markets
- The entity's primary reporting format must be either
  - Business segments
  - Geographical segments

| | Other financial and operational information | | UK GAAP comparison |

| Financial accounting material | IAS 12 Income Taxes | **IAS 14 *Segment Reporting*** | IFRS 8 Operating Segments | IAS 24 Related Party Disclosures |

- Disclosuresrequired for primary reporting format:

  - Segment revenue
  - Segment result
  - Segment assets
  - Segment liabilities
  - Segment acquisition of non-current assets
  - Segment depreciation/amortisation

- More limited disclosure required for secondary reporting format

IFRS 8 *Operating Segments*

- **Segment reporting** is necessary for a better understanding and assesment of:

    - Past performance

    - Risks and returns

- IFRS 8 adopts the **managerial approach** to identifying segments

- The Standard gives guidance on how segments should be **identified** and **what information should be disclosed** for each

- It also sets out requirements for related disclosures about **products and services, geographical areas and major customers**

Note. IAS 14 is still fully examinable but an awareness of IFRS 8 is required as well.

IAS 24 *Related Party Disclosures*

Check the definition if you don't already know it. Key elements are:

> **Substance** of relationship is the key factor.

- Direct or indirect control
- One party has influence
- Common control
- Both parties subject to influence from the same source

Disclose transactions and balances

- Names of the related parties
- Description of the relationship between the parties
- Description of the transactions
- Amounts involved
- Any other explanations required
- Amounts due to/from related parties at the B/S date
- Amounts w/off related party debts

- Disclosure can be in aggregate for similar transactions
- Exemptions for groups and state-centralised enterprises
- Related party transactions are not illegal or suspect, but need to be disclosed for a better understanding

| Financial accounting material | IAS 12 *Income Taxes* | IAS 14 *Segment Reporting* | IFRS 8 *Operating Segments* | IAS 24 Related Party Disclosures |

Other financial and operational information

UK GAAP comparison

Deemed related parties

- Enterprise that directly, or indirectly through one or more intermediaries, control, or are controlled by, or are under common control with, the reporting enterprise
- Associates
- Individuals owning, directly or indirectly, an interest in the voting power of the reporting enterprise that gives them significant influence over the enterprise and close members of the family of any such individual
- Key management personnel
- Enterprises in which a substantial interest in the voting power is owned, directly or indirectly, by any person described in the two previous points or over which such a person is able to exercise significant influence

Deemed to be not-related parties

- Two companies simply because they have a director in common
- Providers of finance, trade unions, public utilities, government departments and agencies in the course of their normal dealings with an enterprise by virtue only of those dealings
- A single customer, supplier, franchisor, distributor or general agent with whom an enterprise transacts a significant volume of business merely by virtue of the resulting economic dependence

Control: the ability to direct the financial and operating policies of an entity with a view to gaining economic benefits from its activities.

| | Other financial and operational information | UK GAAP comparison |

| Financial accounting material | IAS 12 Income Taxes | IAS 14 Segment Reporting | IFRS 8 Operating Segments | IAS 24 Related Party Disclosures |

Other financial and operational information

Directors' Report should include:

- Nature of business
- Names of directors
- Employee policies
- Significant events after the balance sheet date

- R & D activity
- Political/charitable donations
- Purchases of own shares
- Creditor payment policy

| Financial accounting material | IAS 12 *Income Taxes* | IAS 14 *Segment Reporting* | IFRS 8 *Operating Segments* | IAS 24 *Related Party Disclosures* |

Other financial and operational information · UK GAAP comparison

In January 2006, the UK Accounting Standards Board issued a Reporting Statement – **The Operating and Financial Review**. Purpose of the OFR is to allow directors to analyse the business' performance to assist users.

Objectives

- Development and performance during year
- Position at year end
- Main underlying trends
- Future development

Principles

- Directors' perspective
- Members' needs first
- Forward looking
- Complement financial statements
- Comprehensive, balanced and neutral

Disclosures

- Nature, objectives and strategy
- Development and performance
- Resources, risks and uncertainties of relationships
- Position of business

Key performance indicators

Disclose/explain, for each KPI:

- Definition and calculation method
- Purpose
- Source of underlying data
- Quantification or commentary on future targets
- Corresponding amounts
- Changes to KPIs

UK GAAP comparison

- Income statement = profit and loss account

Preparation of profit and loss account covered by FRS 3

- Two types of exceptional item

- Statement of total recognised gains and losses

- Reconciliations of movements in shareholders' funds

- Rate of historical cost profit/losses

- Sub-total for operating profit

- More detailed analysis of discontinued operations on the face of the P&L account

Segment reporting = SSAP 25

- Some exemptions from disclosure
- Equal emphasis on business and geographical segments
- Less disclosure than IAS 14 or IFRS 8

Related party transactions = FRS 8

- Some exemptions from disclosure
- Only material transactions need to be disclosed
- Materiality judged from view of reporting entity and related party
- Slightly different disclosure requirements

3: Non-current assets

For most entities the value of non-current assets, including intangible assets, is a significant figure in their balance sheet and must be valued correctly. Hence this chapter covers a variety of IASs/IFRSs dealing with these areas.

IAS 16 *Property, Plant and Equipment* covers all aspects of accounting for these items, which are most tangible non-current assets.

Probable that future economic benefits associated with the assets will flow to the entity

← **Recognition** →

Cost of asset can be reliably measured

Initial measurement

Purchase price

Import duties

Non-refundable purchase taxes

LESS

Trade discounts/rebates

Directly attributable costs

Site preparation

Delivery/handling

Testing

Professional fees

Other costs

Estimate of dismantling/removal costs and siite restoration *(IAS 37)*

Finance costs *(IAS 23)*

Subsequent expenditure

Same criteria as initial costs. Otherwise do not capitalise but charge to income statement.

Subsequent measurement

Cost model	Revaluation model	Depreciation
■ Cost less accumulated depreciation and accumulated impairment losses	■ Revalued amount (fair value at the date of revaluation) less subsequent accumulated depreciation and impairment losses ■ Revalue sufficiently regularly so carrying amount not materially different from fair value ■ All items of same class should be revalued	■ Systematic basis over useful life reflecting pattern of use of asset's economic benefits ■ Periodic review of useful life and depreciation method and any change accounted for as change in accounting estimate

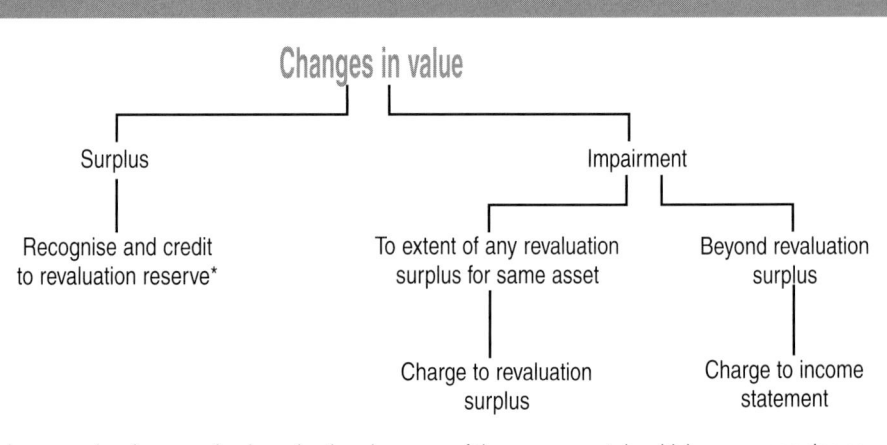

Changes in value

Surplus

Recognise and credit to revaluation reserve*

Impairment

To extent of any revaluation surplus for same asset

Charge to revaluation surplus

Beyond revaluation surplus

Charge to income statement

* Unless reversing a previously recognised revaluation decrease of the same asset, in which case recognise as income to the extent of reversal of the previous decrease.

Definition

An **intangible asset** is an identifiable non-monetary asset without physical substance held for use in the production or supply of goods or services, for rental to others, or for administrative purposes.

Recognition

Recognise if and only if:

- It is probable that the future economic benefits that are attributable to the asset will flow to the entity

- The cost of the asset can be measured reliably

Initial measurement

Intangible assets should initially be measured at cost

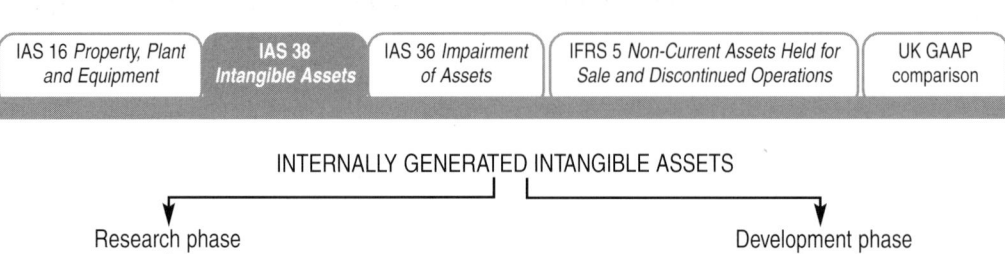

INTERNALLY GENERATED INTANGIBLE ASSETS

Research phase

Recognise as expense when incurred

Development phase

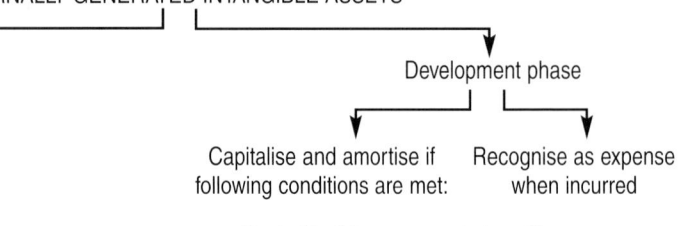

Capitalise and amortise if following conditions are met:

Recognise as expense when incurred

- ▪ **P** robable future economic benefits
- ▪ **I** ntention to complete and use/sell
- ▪ **R** esources adequate to complete and use/sell
- ▪ **A** bility to use/sell
- ▪ **T** echnical feasibility
- ▪ **E** xpenditure can be reliably measured

Internally generated bands, mastheads, publishing titles, customer lists and similar items should not be recognised as intangible assets.

Subsequent expenditure

Subsequent expenditure must meet the original recognition criteria to be added to the cost of the intangible asset.

Amortisation

Should be charged on a systematic basis over the useful life of the asset. Should commence when asset available for use. Period and method to be reviewed at each year end.

Intangibles with indefinite useful life are not amortised, but reviewed at least annually for impairment.

Subsequent re-measurement

Cost model: cost less accumulated amortisation and impairment losses.

Revaluation model: revalued amount less subsequent accumulated amortisation and impairment losses.

Revalued amount is fair value at date of revaluation by reference to an active market.

All other assets in the same class should be revalued unless there is no active market for them, in which case the cost model value should be used for those assets.

Revaluations so that the carrying value does not differ materially from fair value.

Impairment losses

The recoverable amount of the asset should be determined at least at each financial year end and any impairment loss should be accounted for in accordance with IAS 36.

Disclosures

- Distinguish between internally generated and other intangible assets
- Useful lives of assets and amortisation methods
- Gross carrying amount and accumulated amortisation at start and end of period
- Where the amortisation is included in the statement of comprehensive income
- A reconciliation of opening balance to closing balance
- If research and development, how much was charged as expense

Goodwill can be purchased or be acquired as part of a business combination. In either case, the treatment is capitalisation at cost or fair value under IFRS 3.

Negative goodwill

Arises when acquirer's interest in identifiable net assets exceeds the cost of the combination. Results from **errors** or a **bargain.**

Reassess cost of combination and assets.

Recognise **any remaining** goodwill **immediately** in **profit or loss,** that is in the income statement.

Goodwill

Future economic benefits arising from assets that are not capable of being individually identified and separately recognised

Recognise as an asset and measure at cost/excess of purchase cost over acquired interest

Do **not amortise**

Test at least annually for **impairment** (*IAS* 36)

You may be asked to perform a complicated calculation of goodwill as part of a group accounts question.

The aim of IAS 36 *Impairment of Assets* is to ensure that assets are carried in the financial statements at no more than their **recoverable amount**. Note that IAS 36 does not apply to non-current investments held for sale which are covered by IFRS 5.

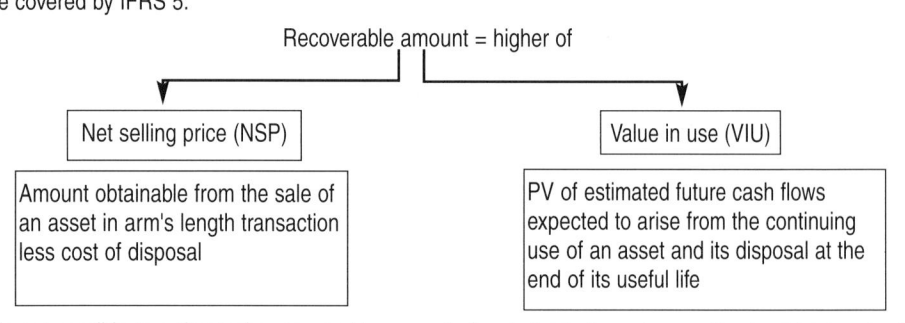

Recoverable amount = higher of

Net selling price (NSP)

Amount obtainable from the sale of an asset in arm's length transaction less cost of disposal

Value in use (VIU)

PV of estimated future cash flows expected to arise from the continuing use of an asset and its disposal at the end of its useful life

Where it is not possible to estimate the recoverable amount of an individual asset, an entity should determine the recoverable amount of the **cash-generating unit** to which it belongs.

The Standard also specifies when an entity should reverse an impairment loss and prescribes certain disclosures for impaired assets.

Indicators of impairment

A review for impairment of a non-current asset or goodwill should be carried out if events or changes in circumstances indicate that the carrying amount of the non-current asset or goodwill may not be recoverable.

External indicators

- Fall in market value

- Change in technological, legal or economic environment

- Increase in market interest rate likely to affect discount rates

- Carrying amount of entity's net assets > market capitalisation

Internal indicators

- Obsolescence or physical damage

- Adverse changes in use

- Adverse changes in asset's economic performance

It may not be possible to associate cash flows with individual assets so the review of the recoverable amount will often have to be applied to **cash generating units** that contain groups of related assets.

Calculation of value in use

Include cash flows	**Exclude cash flows**
■ Directly attributable ■ An appropriate proportion that can be allocated on a reasonable and consistent basis ■ Net cash flows to be received or paid for the disposal of the asset at the end of its useful life on a fair value basis	■ Any future restructuring to which the enterprise is not yet committed ■ Future capital expenditure that will improve/enhance asset in excess of originally assessed standard of performance ■ Financing activities ■ Income tax receipts or payments

The discount rate should be a pre-tax rate that reflects current market assessments of the time value of money and the risks specific to the asset.

Allocation of impairment loss

1 To the goodwill allocated to the cash generating unit (CGU)

2 To all other assets in the cash generating unit on a *pro rata* basis

Recognition of losses

- Assets carried at historic cost – income statement

- Revalued assets – under rules of applicable IAS

- Depreciation adjusted in future periods to allocate the asset's revised carrying amount less residual value over its remaining useful life

Reversal of past impairments

Where the recoverable amount increases, the resulting reversal should be recognised in the current period to the extent that it increases the carrying amount up to the amount that it would have been (net of amortisation or depreciation) had no impairment loss been recognised in prior years.

- **Individual assets**: recognise as income immediately in the statement of comprehensive income unless the asset is carried at revalued amount under another IAS in which case apply the rules of that IAS

- **CGUs**: exact opposite of its original recognition while ensuring that assets are not increased above the lower of their recoverable amount and their carrying amount (after depreciation or amortisation) had there been no impairment loss

- **Goodwill**: not reversed in subsequent period unless:
    - The impairment was caused by a specific external event of an exceptional nature not expected to recur
    - Subsequent external events have occurred which reverse the effect of that event

Disclosures

- The amount of impairment losses recognised in the statement of comprehensive income during the period and the line items affected

- The amount of impairment loss reversals recognised in the statement of comprehensive income during the period and the line items affected

- The amount of impairment losses debited directly against equity in the period

- The amount of impairment loss reversals credited directly to equity in the period for material impairment losses or loss reversals:

  - The events and circumstances

  - The amount

  - The nature of the asset or cash generating unit

  - For initial losses whether recoverable amount is NSP or VIU (and details of basis of selling price or discount rate as appropriate)

IFRS 5 *Non-Current Assets Held for Sale and Discontinued Operations* was published in 2004.

Definitions

Discontinued operation	A component of an entity that either has been disposed of or is classified as held for sale and:
	(a) Represents a separate major line of business or geographical area of operations,
	(b) Is part of a single co-ordinated plan to dispose of a separate major line of business or geographical area of operations, or
	(c) Is a subsidiary acquired exclusively with a view to resale.
Component of an entity	Operations and cash flows that can be clearly distinguished, operationally and for financial reporting purposes, from the rest of the entity
Disposal group	A group of assets to be disposed of (by sale or otherwise) together as a group in a single transaction; *and* liabilities directly associated with those assets that will be transferred in the transaction
Asset held for sale	Its carrying amount will be recovered principally through sale rather than continuing use

Criteria

- The asset (or disposal group) must be available for immediate sale in its present condition, subject only to usual and customary sales terms and
- The sale must be highly probable.
  For this to be the case:
  - The appropriate level of **management** must be **committed** to a plan to sell
  - An **active programme** to **locate a buyer** and complete the plan must have been initiated
  - The asset (or disposal group) must be **actively marketed** for sale at a price that is reasonable in relation to its current fair value
  - The sale should be expected to qualify for recognition as a completed sale **within one year** from the date of classification as held for sale (subject to limited specified exceptions)
  - Actions required to complete the plan should indicate that it is **unlikely** that **significant** changes to the plan will be made or that the plan will be withdrawn

Presentation

Assets and disposal groups (including associated liabilities) classified as held for sale are presented:

- On the face of the balance sheet
- Separately from other assets and liabilities
- Normally as **current** assets and liabilities (not offset)

Measurement

An entity must measure a non-current asset or disposal group classified as held for sale at the **lower of**:

- Carrying amount
- Fair value less costs to sell

Immediately before initial classifications, measure asset per applicable IFRS. Any impairment loss accounted for as normal.

Non-current assets/disposal groups classified as held for sale are **not depreciated**.

Proforma disclosure

XYZ GROUP – INCOME STATEMENT SECTION OF STATEMENT OF COMPREHENSIVE INCOME FOR THE YEAR ENDED 31 DECEMBER 20X7

	20X7	20X6
Continuing operations		
Revenue	X	X
Cost of sales	(X)	(X)
Gross profit	X	X
Other income	X	X
Distribution costs	(X)	(X)
Administrative expenses	(X)	(x)
Other expenses	(X)	(X)
Finance costs	(X)	(X)
Share of profit of associates	X	X
Profit before tax	X	X
Income tax expense	(X)	(X)
Profit for the year from continuing operations	X	X
Discontinued operations		
Profit for the year from discontinued operations	X	X
Profit for the year	X	X
Profit attributable to		
Owners of the parent	X	X
Minority interest	X	X
	X	X

UK GAAP comparison

IFRS 5 Non-Current Assets Held for Sale and Discontinued Operations

IAS 36 Impairment of Assets

IAS 38 Intangible Assets

IAS 16 Property, Plant and Equipment

UK GAAP comparison

- **Property, plant and equipment = FRS 15**

    - Maximum period of five years between valuation

    - Revaluation based upon current value model

    - Impairment loss due to consumption of economic benefits $\Rightarrow$ profit or loss

    - Residual values not adjusted for price changes

- **Intangible assets = SSAP 13 (R&D) and FRS 10**

    - Capitalisation of development expenditure is optional

    - Goodwill is amortised

    - Presumption of maximum life of goodwill/intangibles of 20 years

- **Impairment = FRS 11**
  - Allocation of impairment loss in a CGU to first goodwill, then intangibles, then tangible assets
  - More restrictive regarding realisation of impairment

- **Assets held for sale** – no UK Standard

4: Investment properties, government grants and borrowing costs

This chapter deals with the remaining aspects of accounting for non-current assets.

IAS 40 *Investment Property*

An **investment property** is property (land or building) held to earn rentals or for capital appreciation or both, rather than for:
- Use in the production or supply of goods or services or for administrative purposes
- Sale in the ordinary course of business

Accounting treatment

- Choice of **fair value model** or **cost model**
- **Fair value model**
  - Revalue to fair value at each accounting date
  - Do not depreciate
  - Gain or loss to I/S
- **Cost model**
  - Follow cost model of IAS 16

Note. Leasehold investment properties are accounted for as finance leases

Exceptions

Owner-occupied property or property held for sale to or being constructed for third parties are not investment property (IAS 16, IAS 2, IAS 11 respectively).

Disclosures

- Criteria for classification
- Assumptions in determining fair value
- Use of independent professional valuer
- Rental income and expenses
- Any restrictions or obligations

IAS 20 *Government Grants*

IAS 20 *Accounting for Government Grants and Disclosure of government assistance* requires the following accounting treatment.

Grants related to income

Either show as credit in the income statement (other income) or deduct in reporting the related expense.

Grants related to assets

Treat as deferred income and credit to income statement on systematic rational basis over useful life of asset *or* deduct grant in arriving at carrying value of asset and recognise as income over asset's life by means of reduced depreciation charge.

Disclosures

- Accounting policy

- Nature and extent of grants recognised

- Unfulfilled conditions and other contingencies relating to grants recognised

Recognise only when reasonable assurance that any conditions will be met and monies received

IAS 23 *Borrowing Costs*

The Standard deals with borrowing costs for **self-constructed assets**.

Borrowing costs

Interest and other costs incurred by an entity in connection with the borrowing of funds.

Qualifying asset

An asset that necessarily takes a substantial period of time to get ready for its intended sale or use.

Included in borrowing costs

- Interest on bank overdrafts and short and long term borrowings
- Amortisation of discounts or premiums related to borrowings
- Amortisation of ancillary costs incurred with the arrangement of borrowings
- Finance charges in respect of finance leases under IAS 17
- Exchange differences as far as they are an adjustment to interest costs

Capitalisation is mandatory if the costs are **directly attributable** to the acquisition, construction or production of a qualifying asset.

UK GAAP comparison

- **Investment property = SSAP 19**
  - Must be measured at open market value
  - All gains/losses $\Rightarrow$ Statement of total recognised gains and losses
  - In balance sheet = Investment property revaluation reserve

- **Government grants = SSAP 4**
  - As CA 85 requires non-current assets to be shown at cost, asset-related grants cannot be deducted from cost, so deferred income method must be used

- **Borrowing costs = FRS 15**
  - Borrowing costs capitalised are limited to finance costs as a result of expenditure incurred

Notes

Having covered lesee accounting in your Financial Accounting studies, this chapter looks at lessor accounting and sale and leaseback transactions.

IAS 17 *Leases*

IAS 17 *Leases* standardises the accounting treatment and disclosure of assets held under lease. It follows the **substance over form** principle.

Finance lease	Lease	Operating lease
A lease that transfers substantially all the risks and rewards of ownership of an asset	An agreement whereby the lessor conveys to the lessee in return for rent the right to use an asset for an agreed period of time	A lease other than a finance lease

Accounting treatment

Finance lease	Operating lease
■ Capitalise asset (lower of fair value and present value of minimum lease payment)	■ Charge rentals on a systematic basis over lease period
■ Set up finance lease liability	■ Balance sheet
■ Repayments split between finance charge and capital	– Only accruals/prepayments for rentals
■ Balance sheet	■ Income statement
– Net book value	– Rental expense
– Finance lease liability	
■ Income statement	
– Depreciation	
– Finance charge	

The finance charge included in a finance lease is allocated to the lease periods using one of three methods:

- Straight-line method
- Sum-of-the-digits method
- Actuarial method

The straight-line method is very simple but rarely used in practice. The actuarial method is the best and most scientific method. In order to use the **actuarial** method you need to know the **effective interest rate**.

Lessors – accounting treatment

Finance lease

- Recognise receivable equal to net investment in the lease as a finance lease asset

- Mirror image of lessee's liability plus unguaranteed residual value

- Unguaranteed residual value is portion of residual value of asset not guaranteed by lessee or guaranteed only by party related to lessor

- Finance income recognised reflecting constant periodic rate of return on net investment outstanding

Operating lease

- Assets held for use under operating leases, are recorded as an asset on the B/S and income in the I/S on a straight-line basis unless another systematic basis is more representative

Sale and leaseback transactions

- If leaseback is a *finance lease,* defer book profit/loss and amortise over lease term

  Double entry is:

  Dr   Cash
  Cr   Finance lease liability

  and then as any other finance lease

- If leaseback transaction is an *operating lease;* where SP = sales proceeds; FV = fair value:

  - If SP = FV (an arm's length transaction), recognise any profit/loss immediately

  - If SP < FV, recognise profit/loss immediately *unless* the apparent loss is compensated by future rentals at below market price, in which case defer and amortise

  - If SP > FV, defer the excess over FV and amortise over lease term (ie recognise FV minus Book Value)

- **Operating lease incentives = SIC 15**

  - Lessor provides incentives for lessee to enter lease

Accounting treatment

Lessor

Recognise cost as a reduction of rental income over lease term on straight-line basis.

Lessee

Recognise benefit as reduction of rental expense over the lease term on straight-line basis

UK GAAP comparison

- **Lease accounting = SSAP 21**

    - If, at the inception of the lease, the present value of the minimum lease payments is > 90% of the fair value of the lease, then transfer of risks and rewards is presumed = finance lease

    - Lease of land and buildings treated as one lease – normally an operating lease

    - For lessors total gross earnings allocated on basis of constant rate of return on net cash investment, ie net investment adjusted for other cash flows especially tax

    - Operating lease incentives spread over shorter of lease term and period until next rent review

6: Revenue and construction contracts

Topic List

Financial accounting material

IAS 11 *Construction Contracts*

UK GAAP comparison

The new material for this chapter concerns the accounting treatment of construction contracts.

IAS 18 *Revenue*

Revenue is that which arises in the course of ordinary activities such as that from sales, services provided, interest, royalties and dividends.

Measurement

- **Fair value** of consideration received/receivable. Deferred amounts discounted

- In a sale financed by the seller, any difference between the fair value of the item and the nominal sales value should be accounted for as interest revenue

Includes only those amounts receivable by the entity on its own account. No sales, goods and sales tax (eg VAT) collected by agent to be passed to the principal.

Recognition

Goods	Services
When the following conditions are met:	■ Conditions 3 to 5 as for goods
1 Transfer of significant risks and rewards of ownership (usually legal title)	■ The stage of completion of the transaction at the balance sheet date can be measured reliably and a proportion applied to the revenue
2 No more control over goods sold	■ Interest – time proportion basis (effective yield)
3 Amount of revenue can be reliably measured	■ Royalties – accruals basis
4 Probable that debt will be repaid	■ Dividends – when the right to the dividend is established
5 Transaction costs can be reliably measured	

Disclosure

Accounting policy for each recognition; the amount of each significant category of revenue; amount of revenue from exchange of goods or services.

Construction contracts

A contract specifically negotiated for the construction of an asset or a combination of assets that are closely interrelated or interdependent in terms of their design, technology and function or their ultimate use

Outcome can be estimated reliably

Recognise contract revenue and contract costs by reference to stage of completion of contract

Outcome cannot be estimated reliably

Recognise revenue only to extent of contract costs incurred that it is probable will be recovered. Recognise as expense in period incurred

Any expected loss should be recognised as an expense immediately

Where the outcome of a contract can be estimated reliably, a proportion of contract revenue and costs should be recognised in the income statement by reference to the stage of completion (ie a proportion that fairly reflects the amount of work done).

The stage of completion can be calculated in various ways including:

Proportion of contract costs incurred:	Surveys of work performed:	
$\dfrac{\text{Costs to date}}{\text{Total estimated costs}} \times$ Estimated total revenue/costs	$\dfrac{\text{Work certified}}{\text{Contract price}} \times$ Estimated total revenue/costs	Physical proportion completed

6: Revenue and construction contracts

Disclosures

Income statement	
Revenue (x% × total contract revenue)	X
Expenses (x% × total contract cost)	(X)
	X
Expected loss	(X)
Recognised profit/loss	X

Balance sheet	
Gross amount due from/to customers	
Contract costs incurred	X
Recognised profits less recognised losses	X
	X
Less progress billings to date	(X)
	X/(X)
Trade receivables	
Progress billings to date	X
Less cash received	(X)
	X

The following, not covered above, must also be disclosed under IAS 11 (revised).

- Methods used to determine contract revenue

- Methods used to determine stage of completion of contracts in progress

- Any contingent gains and losses, eg due to warranty costs, claims, penalties or possible losses, in accordance with IAS 37

- Amount of advances received

- Amount of any retentions (progress billings not paid until the satisfaction of certain conditions)

UK GAAP comparison

Revenue

- No UK Standard but principles of FRS 5 are consistent with IAS 18

Construction contracts = SSAP 9

- Gross amount due from customers split into
    - Long-term contract balance in stock
    - Amounts recoverable on contracts in debtors

7: Financial instruments

In recent years there has been a huge growth in the number and complexity of financial instruments available. This chapter considers the accounting requirements for these financial instruments.

Because of the inherent difficulties in this complex area, it is hard for users to assess the nature, amount and cost of an entity's debt and equity resources.

Before IAS 32 and IAS 39 many financial instruments were treated as off-balance sheet finance and invisible to the users of accounts. Because of their significance, the IASB tackled the project in three phases:

- IAS 32 *Presentation* (1995) ensured the user was aware of the instruments and associated risks

- IAS 39 *Recognition and Measurement* (1998) prescribed specific accounting treatment as an interim measure

Both Standards were revised in December 2003.

- IFRS 7 *Disclosure* (2005) effective from 1 January 2007, specifies disclosures required for financial instruments

Definitions

Financial instrument: any contract that gives rise to a financial asset of one entity and a financial liability or equity instrument of another.

Financial asset: cash; equity instrument of another entity; contractual right to receive cash/other financial assets; contract that can be settled in the entity's own equity instruments and may be either a derivative or a non-derivative.

IAS 32 Presentation

- Financial instruments should be classified as either
  - Liability (debt), or
  - Equity
- Compound instruments (exhibiting characteristics of both) must be split into their debt and equity components
- Substance rather than legal form applies (eg redeemable preference shares are a financial liability)
- Interest, dividends, loss or gains relating to a financial instrument claimed as a liability are reported in the I/S, while distributions to holders of equity instruments are debited directly to equity (in the SOCIE)
- Offsetting of a financial asset and liability is only allowed where there is a legally enforceable right and the entity intends to settle net or simultaneously

Financial liability: contractual obligation to deliver cash/other financial asset; contractual obligation to exchange financial instruments under potentially unfavourable conditions.

Equity instrument: contract that evidences a residual interest in the assets of an entity after deducting all its liabilities.

IAS 39 *Recognition and Measurement*

Recognition and derecognition

- Financial instruments should be **recognised** when the entity becomes a **party to the contractual provisions of the instrument**

- **Derecognition**

  - *Financial assets:* where the contractual rights to the cash flows expire or the financial asset is transferred

  - *Financial liabilities:* when obligations expire/are discharged/cancelled

Measurement

- Financial instruments are initially measured at **fair value** plus transaction costs directly attributable to the acquisition or issue

- Transaction costs are included in initial measurement (but not subsequent measurement)

- Financial assets are divided into four types for subsequent measurement:

  - Loans and receivables originated by the entity (and not held for trading)
  - Held-to-maturity investments
  - Financial assets at fair value through profit and loss*
  - Available-for-sale financial assets (any other financial assets)

  * This means either an asset that is held for trading (ie a derivative or a financial asset acquired principally for selling in the near term) or any financial asset that the entity decides upon initial recognition to designate as held at fair value through profit or loss.

Subsequent measurement:
financial assets (FA)

Amortised cost	Fair value
■ Held-to-maturity	■ Financial assets at
■ Loans and	fair value through
receivables	profit or loss
originated by	■ Available-for-sale
entity and not held	financial assets
for trading	(any other)

Subsequent measurement:
financial liabilities (FL)

Fair value	Amortised cost
■ Financial liabilities	■ All others
at fair value	
through profit or	
loss	
■ FL arising when	
transfer of FA	
does not qualify	
for derecognition	

Calculations

The method used in the following example applies to deep discount bonds and other similar instruments (including zero coupon bonds).

Debt issued for $400,000 (nominal) on 1.1.20X1 for proceeds of $315,526; redeemed for $400,000 (ie par) on 31.12.20X5

Interest rate = 4%

Effective interest rate = 9.5%

Annual interest payments (4% × $400,000 × 5)		80,000
Deep discount ($400,000 − 315,526)		84,474
		164,474

At inception	DEBIT	Cash	$315,526	
	CREDIT	Liability		$315,526

Year	I/S charge *	Actual interest payable	Rolled up interest charged to I/S	Closing liability in B/S
20X1	29,975	16,000	13,975	329,501
20X2	31,303	16,000	15,303	344,804
20X3	32,756	16,000	16,756	361,560
20X4	34,348	16,000	18,348	379,908
20X5	36,092	16,000	20,092	400,000
	164,474	80,000	84,474	

*9.5% × opening liability in B/S

Fair value is measured as quoted market price in an active market where possible.

7: Financial instruments

Gains and losses (on remeasurement to fair value)

- Held at fair value: I/S

- Available-for-sale financial assets: reported in equity until disposal, when gain or loss recognised in income statement

Impairment

- Impairment review where evidence of financial asset being impaired

- Original effective interest rate should be used when discounting future cash flows to calculate the impairment

- Impairment loss is charged to I/S

- Where available-for-sale financial asset suffers impairment loss, cumulative losses on fair value adjustments previously recognised in equity are recognised in the I/S as well as impairment loss

- Reversals: I/S

IFRS 7 *Financial Instruments – Disclosure*

The objective of IFRS 7 is to require entities to provide disclosures in their financial statements that enable users to evaluate:

(a) The significance of financial instruments for the entity's financial position and performance

(b) The nature and extent of risks arising from financial instruments to which the entity is exposed and how the entity manages those risks.

This information can influence a user's assessment of the financial position and performance of an entity and of the nature of its future cash flows.

Disclosures

Balance sheet	**Income statement**

- Carrying amount of financial assets and liabilities by IAS 39 category

- Reasons for any reclassification between fair value and amortised cost

- Details of assets and exposure to risk where transfers of assets have taken place

- Net gains/losses by IAS 39 category

- Interest income/expense

- Impairment losses

UK GAAP comparison

IAS 32 = **FRS 25**

IAS 39 = **FRS 26**

IFRS 7 = **FRS 29**

- No examinable differences between IAS/IFRS and FRS

8: Group financial statements

Basic consolidation techniques were covered in the
Financial Accounting *syllabus. In this chapter we*
consider further areas of consolidation and the
accounting treatment of joint ventures.

Consolidated balance sheet

Consolidation technique	Look out for:
Step 1. Establish group structure *Step 2.* Set out net assets of subsidiary *Step 3.* Produce a goodwill working *Step 4.* Calculate minority interest *Step 5.* Calculate consolidated retained earnings.	■ Fair value adjustments ■ Mid-year acquisitions ■ Inter-company loans ■ Unrealised profit ■ Dividends ■ Transfers of non-current assets

Summary: Consolidated balance sheet

Purpose   To show the net assets which P controls and the ownership of those assets

Net assets   Always 100% P plus 100% S providing P holds a majority of voting rights

Share capital   P only

Reason   Simply reporting to the parent company's shareholders in another form

Reserves   100% P plus group share of post-acquisition retained reserves of S less consolidation adjustments

Reasons   To show the extent to which the group actually owns total assets less liabilities

Minority interest MI share of S's consolidated net assets

Reason   To show the extent to which other parties own net assets that are under the control of the parent company

Consolidated income statement

Purpose	To show the results of the group for an accounting period as if it were a single entity
Sales revenue to profit after tax	100% P + 100% S (excluding dividend receivable from subsidiary and adjustments for intra-group transactions)
Reason	To show the results of the group which were controlled by the parent
Intra-group sales	Strip out intra-group activity from both sales revenue and cost of sales
Unrealised profit on intra-group sales	(a) Goods sold by P: increase cost of sales by unrealised profit
	(b) Goods sold by S: increase cost of sales by full amount of unrealised profit and decrease minority interest by their share of unrealised profit
Depreciation	If the value of S's non-current assets have been subjected to a fair value uplift then any additional depreciation must be charged in the consolidated income statement. The minority interest will need to be adjusted for their share

Transfer of non-current assets   Expenses must be increased by any profit on the transfer and reduced by any additional depreciation arising from the increased carrying value of the asset

The **net** unrealised profit (ie the total profit on the sale less cumulative 'excess' depreciation charges) should be eliminated from the carrying amount of the asset and from the profit of the company that made the profit.

For instance, H transfers an asset with a carrying value of £1,000 to S for £1,100. Depreciation is 10% p.a. The net unrealised profit is £90. This is debited to H's income statement and to the carrying value of the asset.

Minority interests   MI% × profit after tax

Mid-year acquisition   Apportion income statement of subsidiary between pre-acquisition and post-acquisition periods.

Associates

Individual investor's books

- Carry at cost, or
- In accordance with IAS 39
- Account for as an available-for-sale financial asset

Balance sheet

Initial cost	X
Add/less: post acquisition share of profits/losses (before dividends)	X/(X)
Less: post-acquisition dividends received to avoid double counting	(X)
Carrying value	X

Consolidated financial statements

Use equity method unless:

- Investment acquired and held exclusively with a view to disposal soon
- Investor ceases to have significant influence

In these cases record at cost.

Income statement

Group share of associate's profit after tax

Note that where the associate makes a **loss** this is recognised in the group income statement and deducted from the carrying value of the associate. When that carrying value is reduced to zero no further losses are recognised.

Disilosals

> **Best practice: Goodwill on acquisition which has not been written off as impaired through the I/S must be included as part of profit/loss on disposal.**

Gain or loss on disposal is calculated as follows.

In holding company

	£
Sales proceeds	X
Less cost of investment	(X)
Profit/(loss)	X/(X)

In group accounts

Either

Sale proceeds		X
Less: net assets now sold	(X)	
goodwill not written off	(X)	
		(X)
Profit/(loss)		X/(X)

Or

Profit/(loss) per holding company	X
Less post-acquisition retained earnings disposed of	(X)
	X
Add goodwill written off	X
	X

Full disposal

- In I/S
  - Consolidated results to date of disposal
  - Show group gain or loss separately before interest
- In B/S: no subsidiary therefore no consolidation or MI

Subsidiary to subsidiary

- MI in I/S will be based on % before and after disposal, ie time apportion
- MI in B/S based on year end %

Subsidiary to associate

- I/S: treat as subsidiary to date of disposal, consolidate for correct no. of months and show MI in that amount. Treat as associate thereafter
- B/S: equity valuation based on y/e holding

Subsidiary to trade investment

- I/S: treat as subsidiary to date of disposal. Show dividend income only thereafter
- B/S: leave investment equity valuation at date of disposal, consider whether any write-down is required

Note. A subsidiary disposed of will be treated as a **discontinued operation** per IFRS 5.

Control

- Control over an entity is key to whether it is a subsidiary
- Can have control with < 50% voting rights
- May need to consider potential voting rights
- A special purpose entity (SPE) should be consolidated if controlled
- Control can be lost through a deemed disposal

Piecemeal acquisition

> A controlling interest in a subsidiary may be built up over a period of time.

Two approaches

- Only take account of the subsidiary when control is achieved (per IAS 27)
- If the company has been equity accounted as an associate, then account for the additional interest separately (the **step-by-step method**)

Suggested method

General rule: pre-acquisition and post-acquisition retained earnings and profits should be established at each purchase of shares.

- Ignore share purchases which keep equity shares <20%; make no step-by-step calculations before the bought company becomes an associate

> This question may not arise; control may be achieved after the first purchase, with a further purchase afterwards.

- When the purchase of shares first takes a company's holding >20% (up to 50%), treat all shares purchased up to this date as a single block of purchases for the calculation of pre-acquisition profits.

- For future (significant) purchases up to the time when control is eventually acquired, the step-by-step method should be applied.

Deferred consideration

- To be payable at a later date
- Measured at fair value at acquisition date
- If payable in cash discounted to present value

Contingent consideration

- May be payable in the future
- Increased as part of cost if:
    - Probable will be paid
    - Can be measured reliably
- If it is cash discounted to present value

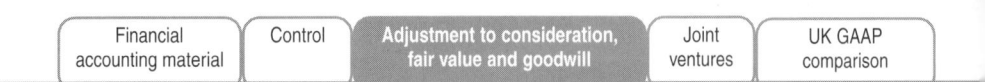

Adjustments to fair value and goodwill

- At acquisition date fair value attributed to:
    - Tangible net assets
    - Intangible assets ⎫
    - Contingent liabilities ⎬ Even if not recognised by acquiree

- Any adjustments to these fair values recognised within 12 months of acquisition are used to alter goodwill figure

Joint ventures

A **joint venture** is a contractual arrangement whereby two or more parties undertake an economic activity which is subject to joint control *(IAS 31)*.

Joint control

Is the contractually agreed sharing of control over an economic activity

Types of joint venture

- Jointly controlled operations
- Jointly controlled assets
- Jointly controlled entities

Accounting treatments

Jointly controlled operations and assets

- No adjustment on consolidation
    - B/S: include all own and appropriate share of joint assets and liabilities
    - I/S: include all own and appropriate share of joint revenue and expenses

Jointly controlled entitles

- Either: proportionate consolidation (line by line basis or by category)
- Or: equity method

UK GAAP comparison

Fair value   =   FRS 7

- FRS 7 is more restrictive in what intangible assets can be recognised than IFRS 3 – only separable intangible assets

Goodwill   =   FRS 10

- Goodwill amortised over useful economic life
- Negative goodwill recognised on balance sheet

Consolidation = FRS 2

- Exclusion of a subsidiary on grounds of severe long-term restrictions
- Potential voting rights considered
- Minority interest presented separately from shareholders' funds

Associates   =   FRS 9

- More detail shown in consolidated profit and loss account
- If share of associate's losses exceed cost ➞ liability

Joint ventures =   FRS 9

- Use gross equity method

9: Earnings per share and distributable profits

Topic List

Basic EPS

Diluted EPS

Distributable profits

UK GAAP comparison

This chapter looks at the calculations for basic and diluted earnings per share and also the UK rules for determining distributable profits.

IAS 33 Earnings per Share

This Standard aims to improve the **comparison** of different entities in the same period and of the same entity in different periods.

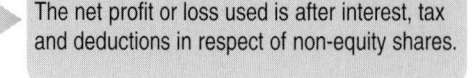

Basic calculation

$$\frac{\text{Net profit/loss attributable to ordinary shareholders}}{\text{Weighted average no. of shares in issue during the period}}$$

The net profit or loss used is after interest, tax and deductions in respect of non-equity shares.

Changes in capital structure

It is necessary to match the earnings for the year against the capital base giving rise to those earnings.

Bonus issue	Issue at full market price	Rights issue
The earnings of the entity will not rise (no new funds injected); to calculate the number of shares:	New capital is introduced therefore earnings would be expected to rise from date of new issue; to calculate the number of shares:	For purposes of calculating the number of shares, treat this as an issue at full market price followed by a bonus issue:
<ul><li>Treat bonus shares as if in issue for the full year</li><li>Apply retrospectively, reducing the reported EPS for the previous year by the reciprocal of the bonus fraction</li></ul>	<ul><li>Use time weighted average number of shares for period</li><li>No retrospective effect</li></ul>	<ul><li>Use weighted average number of shares in issue for the period modified by the retrospective effect of the bonus element</li><li>Bonus element $$\dfrac{\text{Actual cum-rights price}}{\text{Theoretical ex-rights price}}$$</li></ul>

Diluted EPS

Required where a listed entity has outstanding convertible loan notes, preferred shares, debentures, options or warrants.

Must be shown on the face of the income statement and given equal prominence with basic EPS.

- Numerators of calculations must be disclosed. Denominators must be disclosed and reconciled to each other
- Other amounts per share may be shown but profit used must be reconciled to a line item in the income statement

Convertible loan notes or preference shares

- *Earnings*

Net basis earnings	X
Add back loan note interest net of tax (or preference dividends) 'saved'	X
Diluted earnings	$\overline{\overline{X}}$

- *No of shares*

Basic weighted average	X
Add additional shares on conversion (use terms giving max dilution available after y/e)	X
Diluted number	$\overline{\overline{X}}$

Distributable profits

- Based upon individual entity profit not consolidated

- Private company = net accumulated realised profits

- Public company = also deduct net unrealised losses

UK GAAP comparison

EPS   =   FRS 22

- No examinable differences between IAS 33 and FRS 22

10: Financial statement analysis: introduction and ratios

Topic List

Users and user focus

Accounting ratios and relationships

Cash flow statements and their interpretation

The analysis and interpretation of financial statements is an important element of the Financial Reporting *examination and will account for approximately 30% of the marks available.*

Users and user focus

- Present/political investors - profiability/return

- Employees - stability

- Lenders - liquidity

- Suppliers/trade creditors - liquidity

- Customers - stability

- Governments/agencies - taxation

- The public - varied interests

Return on capital employed

$$\text{ROCE} = \frac{\text{PBIT}}{\text{Capital employed}} = \frac{\text{PBIT}}{\text{Total assets less current liabilities}}$$

- When interpreting look for:
  - To how much risk is the business exposed?
  - How capital intensive is it?
  - What ROCE do similar businesses have?
- Problems: which items to consider to achieve comparability:
  - Revaluation reserves
  - Policies, eg goodwill, R&D
  - Bank overdraft: short/long-term liability
  - Investments and related income: exclude
- Examine
  - Change year to year
  - Comparison to similar entities
  - Comparison with current market borrowing rates

Return on equity

$$\text{ROE} = \frac{\text{PAT and pref div}}{\text{Ord share capital + reserves}} \; \%$$

- More restricted view of capital than ROCE, but same principles

Profit margin

$$\text{Profit margin} = \frac{\text{PBIT}}{\text{Sales}}\% \quad \text{Gross profit margin} = \frac{\text{Gross profit}}{\text{Sales}}$$

- Useful to compare profit margin to profit % to investigate movements which do not match

Asset turnover

$$\text{Asset turnover} = \frac{\text{Sales}}{\text{Total assets less current liabilities}}$$

- Measures efficiency of use of assets; can amend to just non-current assets for capital intensive business

10: Financial statement analysis: introduction and ratios

Current ratio

$$\text{Current ratio} = \frac{\text{Current assets}}{\text{Current liabilities}}$$

- Assume assets realised at book value
- 2:1 acceptable? 1.5:1? Depends on industry

Quick ratio

$$\text{Quick ratio (acid test)} = \frac{\text{Current assets - Inventory}}{\text{Current liabilities}}$$

- Eliminates illiquid and subjectively valued inventory
- Could be high if overtrading with rec'bles, but no cash
- 1:1 OK? But supermarkets etc on 0.3 (no rec'bles)

A/cs receivable collection period

$$\frac{\text{Trade receivables}}{\text{Credit sales}} \times 365$$

- Consistent with quick/current ratio? If not, investigate

Inventory turnover/days

$$\text{Turnover} = \frac{\text{Cost of sales}}{\text{Av inv}} \qquad \text{Days} = \frac{\text{Av inv}}{\text{Cost of sales}} \times 365$$

- Higher the better? But remember:
  - Lead times
  - Seasonal fluctuations in orders
  - Alternative uses of warehouse space
  - Bulk buying discounts
  - Likelihood of inventory perishing or becoming obsolete

A/cs payable payment period

$$\frac{\text{Trade accounts payable}}{\text{Purchases}} \times 365$$

- Use cost of sales if purchases not disclosed

Cash cycle

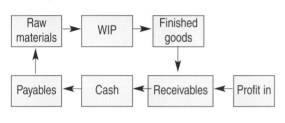

- Cash flow timing $\neq$ sales/cost of sales timing as credit is taken
- Holding inventory delays time between payments for goods to suppliers and sales receipts from customers

Why liquidity changes

- **Credit control efficiency** altered
- Altering **payment** *period of suppliers:* many companies in the recession used their suppliers as a source of funding
- **Inventory control**: in the recession many companies reduced their inventory holdings to maintain their liquidity

In an economic downturn, liquidity becomes a crucial issue.

Example

Think of all those dot.com businesses!

10: Financial statement analysis: introduction and ratios

Gearing

$$\text{Gearing ratio} = \frac{\text{Prior charge capital}}{\text{Total capital}} \%$$

Interest cover

$$\text{Interest cover} = \frac{\text{PBIT (incl int receivable)}}{\text{Interest payable}}$$

- Is interest cover a better way to measure gearing?

  - Company must generate enough profit to cover interest
  - Is 3+ safe? Consider relevance of profit vs cash

Debt/equity ratio

$$\text{Debt/equity ratio} = \frac{\text{Prior charge capital}}{\text{Ordinary share capital and reserves}} \%$$
(> 100% = high)

These ratios deal with long-term liquidity.

There are difficulties in assessing gearing.

- Use of equity accounting to lower gearing

- Elements included are subjective. The following may have an impact.
  - Convertible loan notes
  - Preference shares
  - Deferred tax
  - Goodwill and development expenditure capitalisation
  - Revaluation reserve

These ratios are used by someone contemplating investment. They consider an entity's shares as a source of income (dividends) and/or source of capital growth (share price).

Dividend yield

$$\text{Dividend yield} = \frac{\text{Div per share}}{\text{Mid-market price}} \ \%$$

- Low yield: retains large proportion of profits to reinvest
- High yield: risky company or slow-growing

Dividend cover

$$\text{Dividend cover} = \frac{\text{EPS}}{\text{Net div per ordinary share}} \quad \text{or} \quad \frac{\text{Profit after tax and pref div}}{\text{Div on ordinary shares}}$$

- Shows how safe the dividend is, or extent of profit retention. Variations due to maintaining dividend vs declining profits

P/E ratio

$$\text{P/E ratio} = \frac{\text{Mid-market price}}{\text{EPS}}$$

- Higher the better; reflects confidence of market
- Rise in EPS will cause increase in P/E ratio, but maybe not to same extent: context of market, industry norms

Earnings yield

$$\text{Earnings yield} = \frac{\text{EPS}}{\text{Mid-market price}}$$

- Shows dividend yield if no retention
- Compare entities with different dividend policies
- Shows growth rather than earnings

Indirect method

CASH FLOW STATEMENT FOR YEAR ENDED 31.12.X1

Cash flows from operating activities

Net profit before taxation	X
Adjustments for	
Depreciation	X
Investment income	(X)
Interest expense	X
Operating profit before working capital changes	X
Increase in trade and other receivables	(X)
Decrease in inventories	X
Decrease in trade payables	(X)
Cash generated from operations	X
Interest paid	(X)
Income taxes paid	(X)
Net cash from operating activities	X

> Think carefully about what you are adding and subtracting.

Direct method

Cash recieved from customers	X
Cash payment to suppliers	(X)
Cash paid to and on behalf of employees	(X)
Other cash payments	(X)
Net cash from operating activities	X

Net cash from operating activities brought forward		X
Cash flows from investing activities		
Purchase of property, plant and equipment	(X)	
Proceeds from sale of equipment	X	
Interest received	X	
Dividends received	X	
		(X)
Cash flows from financing activities		
Proceeds from issuance of share capital	X	
Proceeds from long-term borrowings	X	
Payment of finance lease liabilities	(X)	
Dividends paid	(X)	
Net cash used in financing activities		(X)
Net increase in cash and cash equivalents		X
Cash and cash equivalents at beginning of period		X
Cash and cash equivalents at end of period		X

Extra information

Extra information not found in other primary statements.

- Relationships between profit and cash shown
- Cash equivalents are included in cash balances, giving a better picture of the liquidity of the company
- Financing inflows and outflows must be shown, rather than simply passed through reserves

Examining relationships

- Cash flow gearing: compare operating cash flows and financing flows, particularly borrowing
- Operating cash flows to investment flows: match cash recovery from investment to investment
- Investment to distribution: indicates the proportion of total cash outflow designated specifically to investor return and reinvestment

11: Financial statement analysis: interpretation

Topic List

Factors to consider

Non-financial performance indicators

Advanced earnings measures

Limitations

In the previous chapter we considered the role of ratios in understanding financial statements. In this chapter we look at other factors to consider when interpreting financial statements.

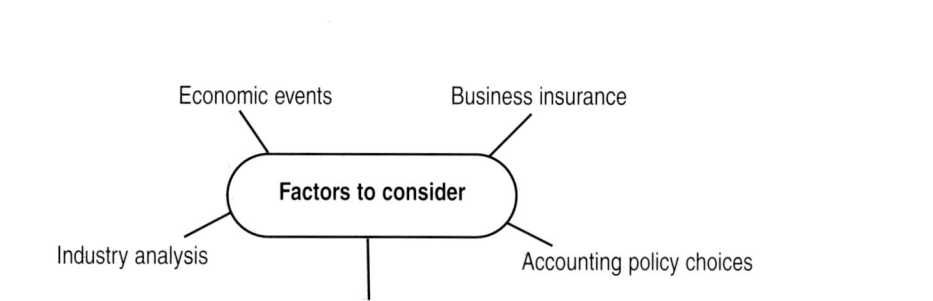

Non-financial measures

- Quality
- Lead times
- Reward
- No. of customer complaints and warranty claims

- Delivery to time
- Non-productive hours
- System/machine down time

The benefit of non-financial indicators is that anything meaningful can be compared.

Advantages

☑ Less easily manipulated

☑ Counteract short-termism

Disadvantages

☒ Can lead to information overload

☒ Managers may pursue detailed operational goals at the expense of long-term strategy

A combination of financial and non-financial indicators is needed.

Advanced earnings measures

Example: EBIT

EBIT = Earnings before interest and tax

Also adjusts for non-recurring income/expenses

Example: EBITA

EBITDA = Earnings before interest, tax, depreciation and amortisation

Example: EBITAR

EBITDAR = EBITDA + operating lease rentals

Limitations of financial analysis

- Availability of comparable information
- Use of historical/out-of-date information
- Ratios are not definitive – they are only a guide
- Need careful analysis; do not consider in isolation
- It is a subjective exercise
- It can be subject to manipulation
- Ratios are not defined in standard form

Limitations of accounting data

- Profit is subjective and may be manipulated by choice of accounting policy
- Seasonal fluctuations
- Window dressing

11: Financial statement analysis: interpretation

Notes

12: Other Standards

This chapter considers the few accounting standards at which we have not yet looked.

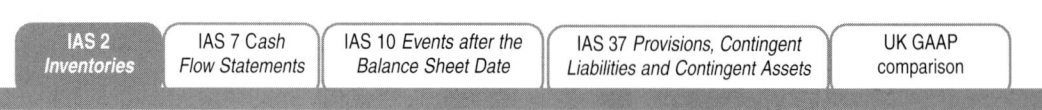

IAS 2 *Inventories*

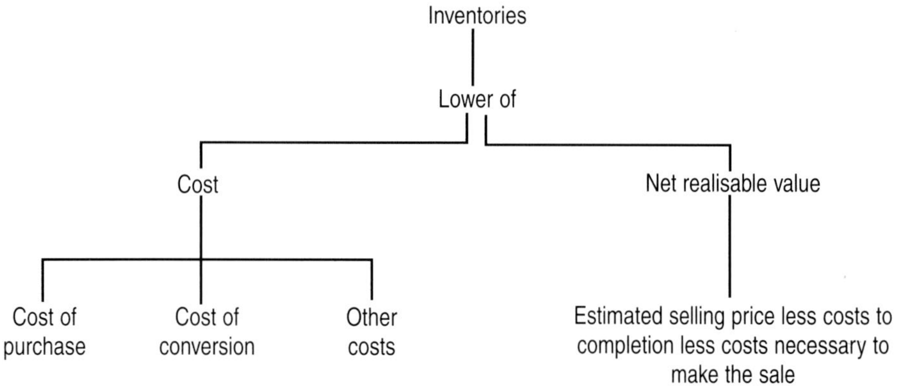

Inventories

Lower of

Cost — Net realisable value

Cost:
- Cost of purchase
- Cost of conversion
- Other costs

Net realisable value:
Estimated selling price less costs to completion less costs necessary to make the sale

Permitted treatment of cost: FIFO or weighted average

LIFO is not permitted under the revised IAS 2 (December 2003)

Indirect method

CASH FLOW STATEMENT FOR YEAR ENDED 31.12.X1

Cash flows from operating activities

Net profit before taxation	X
Adjustments for	
Depreciation	X
Investment income	(X)
Interest expense	X
Operating profit before working capital changes	X
Increase in trade and other receivables	(X)
Decrease in inventories	X
Decrease in trade payables	(X)
Cash generated from operations	X
Interest paid	(X)
Income taxes paid	(X)
Net cash from operating activities	X

> Think carefully about what you are adding and subtracting.

12: Other Standards

CASH FLOW STATEMENT FOR YEAR ENDED 31.12.X1 CONT'D

Net cash from operating activities brought forward		X
Cash flows from investing activities		
Purchase of property, plant and equipment	(X)	
Proceeds from sale of equipment	X	
Interest received	X	
Dividends received	X	
		(X)
Cash flows from financing activities		
Proceeds from issuance of share capital	X	
Proceeds from long-term borrowings	X	
Payment of finance lease liabilities	(X)	
Dividends paid	(X)	
Net cash used in financing activities		(X)
Net increase in cash and cash equivalents		X
Cash and cash equivalents at beginning of period		X
Cash and cash equivalents at end of period		X

Cash equivalents: short-term, highly liquid investments that are readily convertible to known amounts of cash and which are subject to an insignificant risk of changes in value.

Note. Cash and cash equivalents consist of cash on hand and balances with banks, and investments in money market instruments. Cash and cash equivalents included in the cash flow statement comprise the following balance sheet amounts.

	20X1	20X0
Cash on hand and balances with banks	X	X
Short-term investments	X	X
Cash and cash equivalents	X	X

Direct method

The operating activities element of the cash flow statement is different.

Cash flows from operating activities	
Cash receipts from customers	X
Cash paid to suppliers and employees	(X)
Cash generated from operations	X
Interest paid	(X)
Income taxes paid	(X)
Net cash from operating activities	X

Standard workings

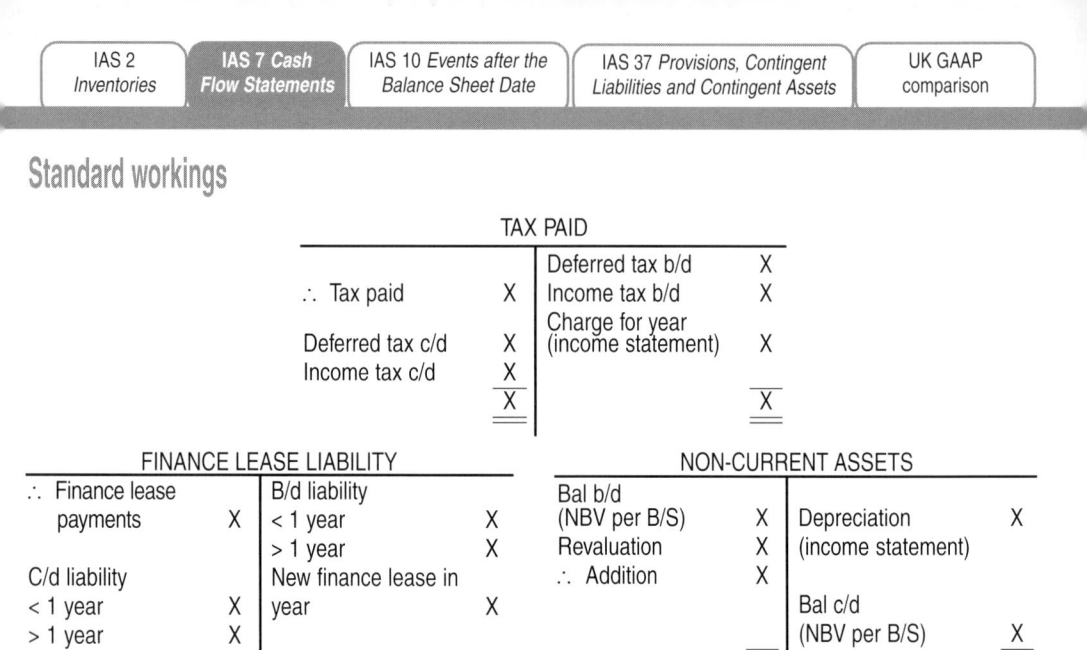

TAX PAID

			Deferred tax b/d	X
∴ Tax paid	X		Income tax b/d	X
			Charge for year (income statement)	X
Deferred tax c/d	X			
Income tax c/d	X			
	X̲			X̲

FINANCE LEASE LIABILITY

∴ Finance lease payments	X		B/d liability	
			< 1 year	X
			> 1 year	X
C/d liability			New finance lease in	
< 1 year	X		year	X
> 1 year	X			
	X̲			X̲

NON-CURRENT ASSETS

Bal b/d (NBV per B/S)	X		Depreciation (income statement)	X
Revaluation	X			
∴ Addition	X			
			Bal c/d (NBV per B/S)	X
	X̲			X̲

Consolidated cash flows

Extra notes are required under investing activities

- Purchase or disposal of subsidiary
- Purchase or disposal of other business units

Minority interest

Only the actual payment of cash, eg dividends, to minorities should be reflected in the cash flow statement. Include under 'cash flows from financing'.

The minority interest share of profit after tax represents retained profit plus dividends paid.

Minority interest brought forward	X
Minority interest carried forward	(X)
	(X)
Income statement: profit	X
Dividend paid	X

Associates

Only the actual cash flows from sales or purchases between the group and the entity, and investment in and dividends from the entity should be included.

- Dividends received should be included as a separate item in 'cash flows from investing activities'.

- Separate disclosure of cash flows relating to acquisitions and investments.

- Separate disclosure of financing cash flows between the reporting entity and equity-accounted investees.

The associate's profit before tax represents retained profit plus dividend plus tax.

Investment brought forward	X
Investment carried forward	X
	(X)
Profit before tax	X
Tax	(X)
	X
Dividend from an associate	X

Acquisition or disposal of a subsidiary

Present as a simple item of cash inflow or outflow

- Cash paid/received as consideration should be shown *net* of any cash transferred as part of the purchase/sale

- Summary note required showing:

  - Total purchase/disposal consideration

  - Portion that was cash/cash equivalents

  - Cash/cash equivalents acquired/disposed

  - Other assets/liabilities acquired/disposed

Events after the balance sheet date

Definition: Events, both favourable and unfavourable, which occur between the B/S date and the date on which the financial statements are authorised for issue.

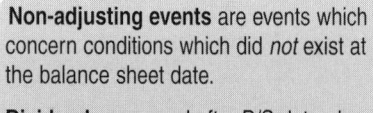

Adjusting events are events after the balance sheet date which provide additional evidence of conditions existing at the B/S date, and therefore need to be incorporated into the financial statements.

Non-adjusting events are events which concern conditions which did *not* exist at the balance sheet date.

Dividends proposed after B/S date: do not adjust but disclose.

An entity should not prepare its financial statements on a going concern basis if the management determines after the balance sheet date either that it intends to liquidate its business, or to cease trading, or that it has no realistic alternative but to do so.

Examples

IAS 37 *Provisions, Contingent Liabilities and Contingent Assets*

IAS 37 *Provisions, Contingent Liabilities and Contingent Assets* was published in 1998 to remedy some abuses of provisions.

- Entities should **not provide** for **costs** that need to be incurred to **operate in the future**, if those **costs could be avoided** by the entity's future actions

- **Costs of restructuring** are to be recognised as a provision only when the entity has an **obligation** to carry out the restructuring

- The **full amount** of any **decommissioning costs** or environmental liabilities should be **recognised from the date on which they arise**

Provision

A liability of uncertain timing or amount. Liabilities are obligations to transfer economic benefits as a result of past transactions or events.

Contingent liability

Should be disclosed unless the possibility of any outflow of economic benefits to settle it is remote.

Contingent asset

Should be disclosed where an inflow of economic benefits is probable.

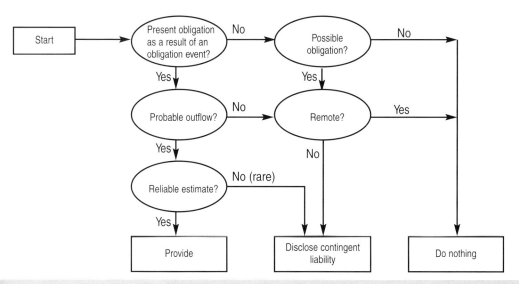

UK GAAP comparison

Inventories = SSAP 9 – no examinable differences

Cash flow statements = FRS 1

- Change in cash only, not cash equivalents
- Nine headings
    - Operating activities
    - Dividends from associates/JVs
    - Returns on investments and servicing of finance
    - Taxation
    - Capital expenditure and financial investment
    - Acquisitions and disposals
    - Equity dividends
    - Management of liquid resources
    - Financing

Events after the balance sheet date = FRS 21 – no examinable differences

Provisions and contingencies = **FRS 12** – no examinable differences

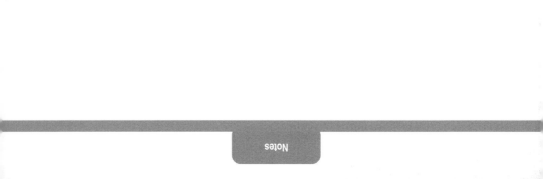
Notes

13: Financial statement analysis: examination techniques

This section extends the interpretation skills of earlier chapters. It wil help you to understand the key aspects of analysis that you may have to address in examinations and how you should approach the examination questions.

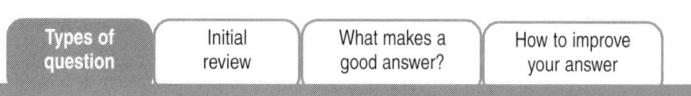

- All questions scenario-based

- All questions in business context to reflect 'real life'

Open-ended questions	Closed-ended questions
- Requirement is unstructured - No parts (a), (b), etc - Will require considerable planning to form structure of answer	- Structured requirements - Parts (a), (b), etc - Each requirement follows on from previous one

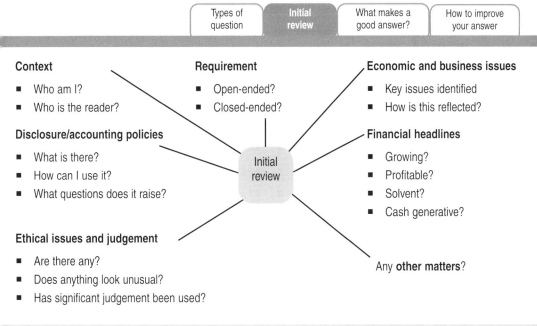

Context

- Who am I?
- Who is the reader?

Disclosure/accounting policies

- What is there?
- How can I use it?
- What questions does it raise?

Ethical issues and judgement

- Are there any?
- Does anything look unusual?
- Has significant judgement been used?

Requirement

- Open-ended?
- Closed-ended?

Initial review

Economic and business issues

- Key issues identified
- How is this reflected?

Financial headlines

- Growing?
- Profitable?
- Solvent?
- Cash generative?

Any **other matters**?

What makes a good answer?

- Plan Structure
  - Key issues
  - Logical order
- Good points
  - Concise
  - Include succinct financial information
  - Reach conclusion from information given
- Points must pass 'because' test
  - This means they demonstrate what has changed and why
- Technical excellence
- Accurate quantification
- Discussion of a range of factors
- Demonstrate higher skills – synthersise, intergrate, analyse, evaluate

How to improve your answer

- Specfic not generic comments – relate to scenario

- Create, don't repeat – don't just repeat figures/comments from the question

- Use 'because' rule to add value

- Reader not writer – focus on information needs of reader

- Intergration not isolation – link information/ratios together

- Use the clues – use information given other than the financial statements

- Big picture – concentrate on big issues not trivia

- Three course meal – introduction, main body, conclusion

Notes

Notes

Notes

13: Financial statement analysis: examination techniques

Notes